My First Animal Kingdom Encyclopedias

AMPHIBIANS

by Emma Carlson Berne

Consultant: Jackie Gai, DVM
Wildlife Veterinarian

CAPSTONE PRESS
a capstone imprint

A+ Books are published by Capstone Press,
1710 Roe Crest Drive, North Mankato, Minnesota 56003
www.mycapstone.com

Library of Congress Cataloging-in-Publication data is available on the Library of Congress website.
ISBN 978-1-5157-3926-5 (library binding)
ISBN 978-1-5157-3937-1 (paperback)
ISBN 978-1-5157-3966-1 (eBook PDF)

Summary: A photo-illustrated reference guide to amphibians that highlights physical features, diet, life cycles, and more.

Editorial Credits
Kathryn Clay, editor; Rick Korab and Juliette Peters, designers;
Kelly Garvin, media researcher; Gene Bentdahl, production specialist

Photo Credits
Minden Pictures: Daniel Heuclin/NPL, 21 (top), Greg Harold/Auscape, 27 (middle), Karl Van Ginderdeuren, 26 (m), Mark Moffett, 31 (top left), Michael & Patricia Fogden, 30 (top right), 31 (bottom right), Nick Garbutt, 30 (br), Piotr Naskrecki, 22-23, Stephen Dalton, 14 (bottom), Uncatalogued/NPL, 31 (tr); National Geographic Creative/Zigmund Leszczynski/Animals Animals/Earth Scenes, 25 (t); Newscom/Europics, 21 (b); Science Source/Dante Fenolio, 23 (inset); Shutterstock: Aggie 11, 32, Anneka, 27 (b), Bildagentur Zoonar GmbH, 12 (inset), Blincov Denis, 8 (b), Brian Lasenby, 17 (t), Cathy Keifer, 17 (m), Chris Hill, 14 (t), Chrystal Bilodeau, 9 (t), davemhuntphotography, 7 (b), 10 (b), 11 (t), 24-25, Dirk Ercken, 5 (inset), 19 (m), 30 (bottom left), Dr. Morley Read, back cover, 11 (b), 18-19, 27 (t), Elena Elisseeva, 1 (bkg), Eric Isslee, 11 (m), 19 (b), Fabio Maffei, 1, (l), FloridaStock, 16 (t), Galyna Andrushko, 8 (t), Goran Bogicevic, 13, guentermanaus, 28 (b), Horia Bogdan, 7 (m), Hurley Z, cover, (bl), Ian Grainger, 12, iliuta goean, 9 (b), Jason L. Price, 16 (b), JIANG HONGYAN, 19 (t), kay roxby, 13 (inset), kurt_G, 30 (tl), llona Koeleman, 29 (b), Luc stacey, 26 (t), Maksimillian, 15 (b), Manuel Findeis, 6 (b), Matt Jeppson, 17 (b), Matt Knoth, 10 (t), mexrix, 6-7, Nashepard, 6 (t), Olga Axyutina, 30-31, Peter Gudella, 8-9, Ralu Cohn, 10-11, Randimal, 31 (bl), reptiles4all, 7 (t), 25 (b), Rosa Jay, 21 (m), 26 (b), Rudmer Zwerver, cover, (br), Sogodel Vlad, 14-15, Spasta, 16-17, Spooner, 9 (m), Susan Schmitz, cover, (tr), tcareob72, 15 (t), Tremor Photography, 20-21, Vadym Zaitsev, 29 (t), Vahan Abrahamyan, 28-29, Vitalii Hulai, 1 (r), Violart, 4-5, Vladimir Efimov, 26-27, worldwildlifewonders, cover (tl)

Artistic Elements: Shutterstock: Olga Axyutina, moj0j0, wawritto

Printed in the United States of America.
082017   010719R

TABLE OF CONTENTS

What Are Amphibians?

Amphibians (am-FI-bee-uhnz) are a group of animals that can breathe through their skin. They spend part of their lives in water and part on land. They have a backbone and no scales. Frogs, toads, and salamanders are amphibians.

class
a smaller group of living things; amphibians are in the class Amphibia

phylum
(FIE-lum)
a group of living things with a similar body plan; amphibians belong to the phylum Chordata (kawr-DEY-tuh); mammals, fish, and reptiles are also in this group

kingdom
one of five very large groups into which all living things are placed; the two main kingdoms are plants and animals; amphibians belong to the animal kingdom

order
a group of living things that is smaller than a class; there are three orders of amphibians

cold-blooded
also called ectothermic (EK-tuh-THER-mik) cold-blooded animals have a body temperature that is the same as the air or water around them; amphibians and reptiles are cold-blooded

species
(SPEE-sees)
a group of animals that are alike and can produce young with each other; there are about 6,500 species of frogs and toads

vertebrate
(VUR-tuh-brit)
an animal that has a backbone; amphibians are vertebrates

reptile
a cold-blooded animal with a backbone and dry scales or bony plates

Getting into Groups

There are more than 7,000 kinds of amphibians. Scientists have divided them into groups. Here are some of the most common.

salamander

an animal with a slender body, four legs, and a long tail; salamanders have smooth, damp skin

frog

an animal with a short body, no tail, and strong back legs; frogs have damp skin

caecilian
(see-SIL-ee-uhn): a legless, wormlike animal; caecilians have poisonous skin and sharp teeth for catching food

newt
(NOOT): a type of salamander with dry, warty skin; newts live in shady forests or under rocks

toad
an animal that looks like a frog but has dry skin

Home, Sweet Home

Amphibians live all around the world. They can be found both on land and in water.

rain forest
a thick area of trees where rain falls almost every day; more than 400 types of amphibians live in the Amazon rain forest

semiaquatic
(SEM-eye-a-KWA-dik) relating to animals that spend some of their time living in water; all amphibians live in water at least part of their lives

habitat
the type of place and conditions in which a plant or animal lives; amphibians live in many different habitats, including forests, rain forests, and deserts

wetland
an area made up of marshes or swamps; wetlands are home to the American Bullfrog

freshwater
water that does not contain salt; amphibians live in freshwater bodies such as rivers, streams, ponds, and lakes

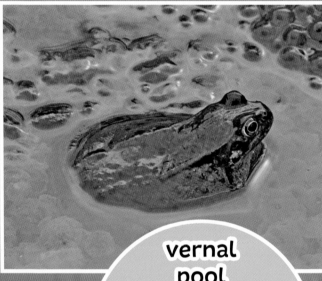

desert
(DEH-zuhrt)
a dry area that gets little rain; the Sonoran Desert toad lives in deserts

vernal pool
(VUR-nuhl POOL)
a shallow area of rainwater in which frogs sometimes lay their eggs

Super Special Skin

Amphibians have special skin. They breathe through it. They can even ooze poison through it to keep away enemies. Amphibians must keep their skin wet. If it dries out, the animals will die.

skin
the layer of tissue that covers and protects an animal's body; amphibians breathe through their skin

scaleless
having no scales; unlike reptiles and fish, amphibians do not have scales

camouflage
(KA-muh-flahzh): coloring that makes animals look like their surroundings; some amphibians blend in with the plants around them

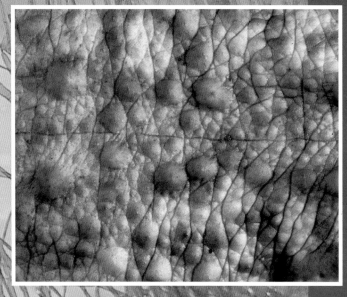

mucus

(MYOO-kus): a slimy substance that covers the bodies of most amphibians; mucus keeps their bodies damp and protected from heat

permeable

(PUR-me-a-bul): allowing liquids or gases to pass through; amphibians have permeable skin—poison and water can seep out of the body, while water and oxygen seep in

poison

a harmful substance that causes sickness or death if touched or eaten; salamanders make a poison that spreads onto their skin

toxin

another word for poison; some amphibians use toxins to keep hungry enemies away

From Egg to Adult

Most amphibians start as eggs.
The eggs hatch into tadpoles.
Soon the young animals
grow into adults.

tadpole
the larval stage
for frogs and toads;
tadpoles live in water
and look like small fish
with pointy tails and big
heads; they have gills
instead of lungs

life cycle
the series of
changes that take
place in a living thing,
from birth to death; the
life cycle for most
amphibians starts
with an egg

larval stage
(LAR-vuhl staj): the
time during which an
amphibian hatches from
its egg and begins moving,
growing, and eating; amphibians
in the larval stage often look
very different from
the adults they
will become

egg
amphibians
lay eggs with a
soft skin covering
instead of a hard shell;
eggs are usually
laid in water in
big clumps

froglet

the next stage of growth for a frog after the larval stage; froglets look like tiny adult frogs

metamorphosis

(met-uh-MOR-fuh-sis) the process of changing from a young animal to an adult animal; during metamorphosis, frogs grow legs and lose their tails; they also lose their gills and grow lungs

gill

a body part used to breathe underwater; some amphibians develop both lungs and gills as they grow; others have only lungs when they are adults

life span

the number of years a certain animal usually lives; some frogs live for only one or two years; most salamanders can live for 10 years

13

Sleeping and Waking

Amphibians are active during the warm months of spring and summer. They go into a deep sleep when fall and winter come. They seem almost dead, but they're not! They "wake up" when warm weather returns.

nocturnal

(nok-TUR-nuhl): active at night; bullfrogs are nocturnal

dormant

(DOOR-ment): slowed down, as if in a deep sleep; amphibians slow their heartbeats and lower their body temperature during winter

hibernate

(HYE-bur-nate): to spend the winter months in a deep sleep; many amphibians hibernate in mud or under logs and leaves

burrow
a tunnel or hole in the ground made or used by an animal; some toads dig into the ground during winter

thaw
to unfreeze; when the weather turns warmer, amphibians thaw from their hibernation

antifreeze
a substance that helps keep liquid from freezing; frogs can make antifreeze in their own blood

Dinner Time

Amphibians eat other animals. What's on the menu? Insects, fish, small mammals—and other amphibians!

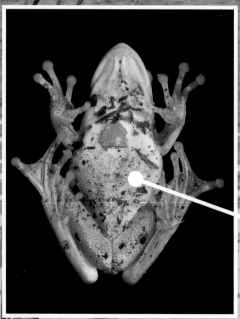

predator
(PRED-uh-tur): an animal that hunts other animals for food; amphibians are predators, but they also have predators of their own, such as birds, snakes, and raccoons

prey
(PRAY): an animal hunted by another animal for food; insects, birds, rodents, spiders, and worms are common prey for amphibians

drinking patch
an area of skin on a frog's belly and thighs that absorbs water

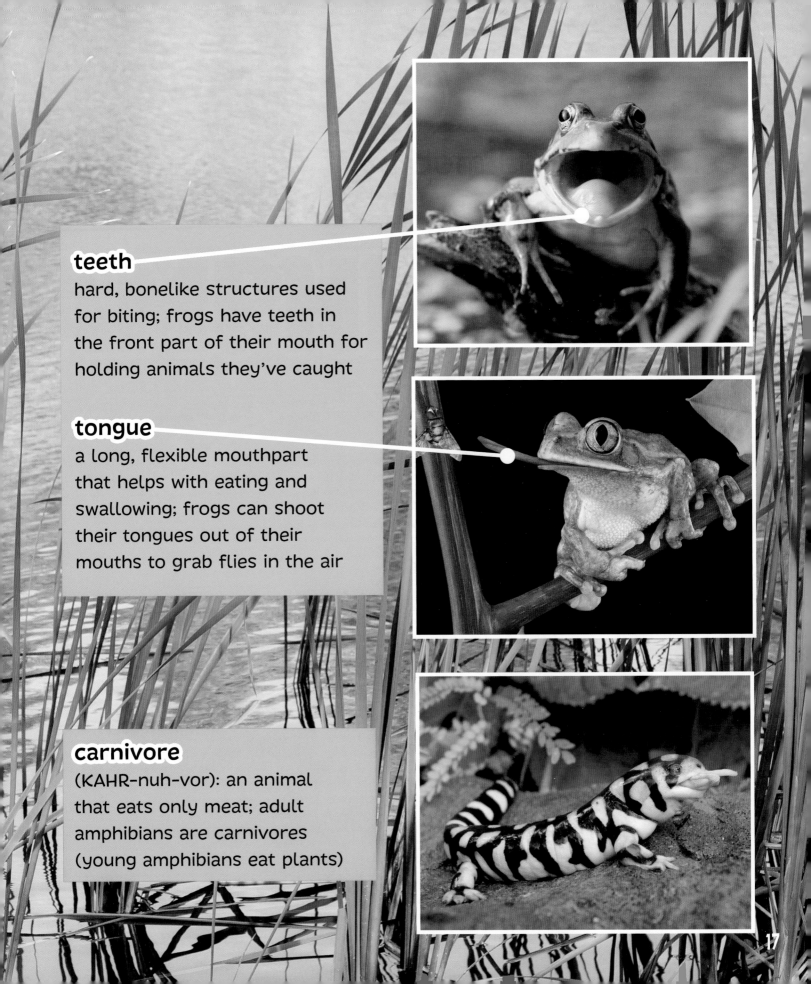

teeth
hard, bonelike structures used for biting; frogs have teeth in the front part of their mouth for holding animals they've caught

tongue
a long, flexible mouthpart that helps with eating and swallowing; frogs can shoot their tongues out of their mouths to grab flies in the air

carnivore
(KAHR-nuh-vor): an animal that eats only meat; adult amphibians are carnivores (young amphibians eat plants)

Featuring Frogs

tree frog
any frog that has a claw-shaped bone in its feet; sticky toe pads help them climb trees

leg
a limb on which an animal stands; frogs have large, powerful back legs; some frogs can hop up to 7 feet (2.1 meters)

toe pad
a sticky, flat, round spot on the bottom tip of a frog's toe; toe pads help frogs climb

third eyelid

a layer of skin that a frog uses to protect its eyes; the skin of the third eyelid is see-through

croak

a deep, throaty sound; frogs croak by pushing air through their voice boxes

bullfrog

the largest frog in North America; bullfrogs are dark green or brown and can weigh more than 1 pound (0.5 kilograms)

poison frog

a kind of colorful frog with poison under its skin; the bright color warns other animals to stay away; also called poison arrow frogs and poison dart frogs

common frog

a medium-sized frog with a gray, green, or brown body and a white underbelly

Salamander Spotlight

fire salamander
a black and yellow salamander that can spray poison at its enemies

lungless
without lungs; some salamanders, such as ensatinas, do not have lungs; they breathe through their skin and mouth only

tail
the backmost part of some animals; salamanders are the only adult amphibians that have tails

mudpuppy

a type of salamander named after the barking noise it makes; mudpuppies are the only salamanders that make noise

siren

a type of salamander that has lungs, gills, and only one pair of legs; sirens use their strong, long tails to swim like fish

webbed feet

fingers and toes that are connected with a thin flap of skin; webbed feet help some salamanders swim

Chinese giant salamander

the largest salamander and the largest amphibian in the world; it can reach nearly 6 feet (1.8 meters) long

Celebrating Caecilians

annuli
(AN-yuh-lie)
ring-shaped skin folds; caecilians are covered with annuli that make them look like worms

gland
a small organ in the body that makes certain chemicals; poisonous glands in a caecilian's skin help protect the animal from predators

tropical
relating to the area around the equator; caecilians live mostly in hot tropical areas

tentacle
a narrow, flexible body part for grabbing or sensing; caecilians are the only amphibians with tentacles

latch
to take hold of or attach to; caecilians use their needlelike teeth to latch onto prey and swallow it whole, not to chew it

eyeless
without eyes; many caecilians do not have eyes

snout
the long front part of an animal's head; caecilian snouts are pointy for digging through dirt and mud

23

Totally Toads

wart
a bump on the skin; the warts on toads are glands that release poison

parotid gland
(puh-ROT-id gland) the organ on a toad that releases poison

common toad
a toad that can change its skin color from brown to green to gray; like many toads, they live near water only when they are producing young

bufotoxin
(BUFF-oh-tok-sin) the poison produced by toads; bufotoxin can make predators sick and irritate people's skin

oak toad

the smallest toad species in North America; it measures only about 1 inch (2.5 centimeters)

cane toad

a large toad that weighs almost 3 pounds (1.4 kilograms); cane toads can make enough poison to kill a person

Weird and Wonderful

Simply put, some amphibians are odd. But what makes them weird also makes them wonderful!

axolotl
(AX-oh-la-tul): also called the Mexican walking fish; this salamander lives in only one lake system in Mexico; it keeps its gills and fins as an adult and can regrow body parts

cave-dwelling olm
a type of salamander that lives in very dim caves; it can go up to 10 years without food

Kaiser's spotted newt
a rare salamander from Iran that hibernates underground for most of the year; during the rainy season it comes out to eat and mate

glass frog
a tiny tree frog whose beating heart and other organs can be seen through its see-through skin

Australian rocket frog
also called the striped rocket frog; it can leap up to 13 feet (4 meters)

ornate horned frog
also called the Pac-Man frog because of its large mouth; it can swallow birds, mice, and other frogs whole

Amphibians and the World

Amphibians are helpful. They play an important part as both predators and prey. They also give us clues about the health of our world.

food web
a system of food chains that affect each other; many species depend on amphibians for food; amphibians also eat insects that carry diseases to humans

ecosystem
(EE-koh-sis-tum)
the connections between plants, animals, and the earth that make up the living world

habitat destruction
when an animal's home is destroyed; amphibians lose their homes when forests are cut down and wetlands are drained to make room for cities

pollution
the presence or introduction of a substance that has harmful effects; because frogs absorb chemicals in their skin, humans can tell if air or water is polluted by studying frogs

extinct
(ek-STINGKT)
no longer living; an extinct animal is one that has died out, with no more of its kind on Earth; up to 30 percent of all amphibian species are now in danger of going extinct

biomass
(BI-oh-mass)
the amount of living things in one area; amphibians have a large biomass in many damp habitats

Fun Facts

Scientists can't figure out if **frogs sleep**. Frogs close their eyes and stay very still. But no one knows if they're really sleeping!

The female **pygmy marsupial frog** never leaves her eggs. She wears them in a pouch just under her skin.

Some amphibians **leak poison** from their skin. Others can actually squirt the poison. They usually aim for a predator's eyes.

The **Malagasy rainbow frog** is one of the rarest frogs in the world. It can live underground for up to 10 months at a time. It is found only in Madagascar.

Goliath frogs are the largest frogs in the world. They can grow up to 12.5 inches (32 centimeters) long and weigh up to 7 pounds (3.2 kilograms). That's about the size of a small cat!

Baby caecilians eat parts of their mother after they are born. They tear off chunks of her skin with their sharp teeth. But it doesn't hurt her. She grows this skin just for them.

Don't eat a **rough-skinned newt**! Its skin, muscles, and blood are full of deadly poison.

The **Darwin's frog** has a special way to keep its babies safe after they hatch. As soon as the tadpoles are born, the male frog swallows them! He keeps them safe in a pouch in his throat. When the tadpoles become little frogs, they jump out.

READ MORE

Bodden, Valerie. *Frogs. Amazing Animals.* Mankato, Minn.: Creative Education/Creative Paperbacks, 2016.

Jackson, Demi. *Name That Amphibian! Guess That Animal!* New York: Gareth Stevens Publishing, 2017.

Plattner, Josh. *Salamander. Animal Superpowers.* Minneapolis: Super Sandcastle, an imprint of Abdo Publishing, 2016.

INTERNET SITES

FactHound offers a safe, fun way to find Internet sites related to this book. All of the sites on FactHound have been researched by our staff.

Here's all you do:
Visit *www.facthound.com*
Type in this code:
9781515739265

Super-cool stuff!

Check out projects, games and lots more at
www.capstonekids.com